CULINARY TOURISM: THE HIDDEN HARVEST

*A Dozen Hot and Fresh Reasons How Culinary Tourism
Creates Economic and Community Development*

Erik Wolf, President and CEO
International Culinary Tourism Association
http://www.culinarytourism.org
4110 SE Hawthorne Blvd #440
Portland, Oregon 97214 USA
Phone   (+1) 503-750-7200
Fax   (+1) 503-296-2447
info@culinarytourism.org

KENDALL/HUNT PUBLISHING COMPANY
4050 Westmark Drive   Dubuque, Iowa 52002

Cover design by Lia Miternique

Copyright © 2006 by Erik Wolf and the International Culinary Tourism Association.

ISBN 0-7575-2677-2

Printed in the United States of America
10 9 8 7 6 5 4 3 2 1

Dear Reader:

Eat, drink and be happy! If life were only that simple. In today's complicated world, we constantly seek new ways to escape. One way is through the universe of culinary delights. Getting to know another culture through travel, and subsequently through local food, is one of the best educational opportunities available to us, yet one of the most undervalued.

I have had the good fortune to travel to many places. At each stop, I made a point to seek out local food and drink. From authentic Hungarian goulash in Budapest to avocado juice in Brazil and the myriad varieties of laksa in Singapore, food and travel have always been intertwined in my life. Friends, even friends of friends, regularly call me to ask where to dine in Sydney, or to recommend an unusual, delicious wine from an obscure part of the world for no more than USD 20. Eating and drinking are universal activities to which everyone can relate. No matter where we were born or live, most of us enjoy a tasty meal or flavorful beverage. This book is based on both research and personal observations drawn from my nearly 20 years of travel industry marketing work, extensive worldwide travel, and countless interviews. My investigation suggested that food and drink are the most overlooked components of the travel experience, and I am convinced they still offer the greatest potential for further development in the global tourism industry.

While researching this book, which originally debuted as a white paper in the summer of 2002, I was amazed to discover that this was, in fact, the first business discussion of Culinary Tourism. Despite its relatively recent arrival, the field has been growing by leaps and bounds. Even so, it appears that the majority of destinations and businesses do not yet fully understand Culinary Tourism's potential. Many have tried to define Culinary Tourism as simply eating out or visiting wineries, and nothing more. Others confuse it with agritourism. Most chefs with whom I spoke recognized their business as providing food and little else. Chefs are artists and are comfortable in the kitchen. Most chefs and restaurateurs did not seem to realize that they are part of the larger tourism ecosystem. Ironically, some of the world's best restaurants are located in hotels. Through additional research, it became painfully evident that there was, and continues to be, a major disconnect between the food and beverage (F&B) and tourism industries. The purpose of this book is to help diminish that gap and bring Culinary Tourism consciousness to the actionable level.

This book provides a wake-up call to F&B and travel professionals throughout the world: Culinary Tourism is an important new niche with important economic and community impacts. I hope to provoke thought, incite discussion, grow industry knowledge and move professionals to find ways to include Culinary Tourism in their own product development and marketing strategies. This book is a starting point on which to build your culinary tourism development efforts. Note that what follows is a candid discussion of the potential for the Culinary Tourism niche and not an implementation plan for a Culinary Tourism strategy.

If, after reading *Culinary Tourism: The Hidden Harvest*, you wish to learn more about Culinary Tourism, I invite you to join our growing family dedicated to the advancement of this industry. Please visit http://www.culinarytourism.org to learn how you can benefit from membership in the Association, or by attending one of our educational events.

Thank you for your interest in Culinary Tourism. Eat well, and travel better!

Sincerely,

Erik Wolf
info@culinarytourism.org
President and CEO, International Culinary Tourism Association

PS. Admittedly, many examples cited herein are from the U.S. state of Oregon and the country of Canada. These two leading areas in the development and promotion of Culinary Tourism offer some of the best examples to illustrate the points herein. We are always looking for solid new examples so feel free to send us yours for possible inclusion in a future edition.

"There is no sincerer love than the love of food."
George Bernard Shaw (1856–1950)

Courtesy of Quebec City Tourism

CONTENTS

ACKNOWLEDGMENTS

It took nearly 20 years of investment in education, professional training and personal development, to arrive at a point in my life where the development of the culinary tourism industry became possible. I cannot take all the credit and would like to acknowledge those individuals who positively nurtured the seeds of Culinary Tourism within me:

- Linda Bell. Thanks for your support and belief in the vision.

- Debra Copeland. Thanks for your never ending stream of creative ideas, support, good karma and love.

- C. Michael Hall, author of *Food Tourism Around the World*. Thanks for your groundbreaking work on culinary tourism, and for your help in getting the world out about Culinary Tourism to the academic community around the world.

- Melody Johnson. Thanks for your ideas, time, support and love.

- Don Monsour, the Association's chairman of the board and a very astute businessman who always keeps me on my toes. Thanks for giving me the benefit of your business acumen developed from your years of experience, as well as your unending patience and guidance.

- Sharyl Parker. Thanks for your omnipresent smile—a source of energy that drives me forward.

- Deborah Wakefield and Barbara Steinfeld. Thanks for believing in the vision and your generosity of time and support.

- Richard and Judy Wolf, my parents. Thanks for taking your honeymoon in New Orleans (a foodie destination by anyone's definition), thereby instilling in me, nine months later, a passion for good food.

- Harry Wolf, my grandfather. Thanks for instilling in me a passion for travel, and for making my education possible.

• The ICTA and OCTA Boards of Directors—Thanks for your ongoing support of, and belief in, my work and the potential of both Associations.

• My beloved colleagues and friends in Oregon: Thanks for your support of, and belief in, my work in Oregon, one of the most beautiful and special places on the planet.

• And a special thanks to all of my other culinary tourism friends and colleagues throughout the world, whose names I cannot list for lack of space, but you know who you are.

EAT WELL, TRAVEL BETTER!

EXECUTIVE SUMMARY

A new niche—*Culinary Tourism*—is slowly but surely sweeping the world's travel industry. Simply put, Culinary Tourism is the development and promotion of prepared food/drink as an attraction for visitors. The reach of Culinary Tourism is broad and encompasses food/drink events, cooking schools and groceries as much as it does restaurants and wineries. Price is not necessarily indicative of quality. Contrary to what some might believe, true Culinary Tourists are not elitists; rather, they are first and foremost explorers who also happen to be impassioned aficionados of food and drink. Culinary Tourism includes all of the *unique and memorable* gastronomic experiences, not just those that have earned four stars or better.

Culinary Tourism has been taken for granted for a long time, and understandably so. As eating and drinking are part of our everyday activities, who would have thought to examine eating/drinking as a separate tourism activity? According to research provided by the (U.S.) National Restaurant Association, more than two-thirds

of table service restaurant operators reported that tourists are important to their business.[1] Culinary Tourists can bring millions of dollars worth of direct and indirect spending to (i.e., investment in) a destination. Culinary Tourism can enhance a destination's product mix, help define unique positioning vis-à-vis other destinations, make significant contributions to a community's economic development and help improve the quality of life for residents.

Professionals in the food/beverage or tourism industries who feel that they have a compelling culinary product, or who are simply curious about how Culinary Tourism could exist in their region, should read on to discover what Culinary Tourism is and the benefits of integrating Culinary Tourism into their destination marketing and product mixes.

This book will help readers "take away" an understanding of the new phenomenon of Culinary Tourism and how it can benefit food and beverage providers, travel industry professionals, communities, and tourists.

What Is Culinary Tourism?

People have traded since the beginning of time for various types of food and drink. The ancient Egyptians, Jews, Greeks and Romans traveled near and far to bring exotic and different foodstuffs to their homes.

The act of eating has always been an international language that we all speak, regardless of where we were born. The history of food and sharing a meal or "breaking bread" together, is important. Whether or not visitors are offered "hospitality," or something to eat and drink, makes an important statement about their value in the host community. The rules of sharing "hospitality" change by community and by culture. Cuisine has a very important potential role in international communication, international education, and international trade.

Have you ever driven an hour or two just to try a new restaurant? Perhaps you have found yourself lost for hours in the aisles of a foreign grocery store while overseas on a business trip. Do you ever schedule your vacations/holidays around food festivals or seasonal fruits and vegetables? If so, you are probably a Culinary Tourist.

"Culinary Tourism" is a newly defined niche that intersects and impacts both the travel and food/beverage industries, which have long been entwined. This relatively new term was first coined by academician Lucy Long in 1998 to express the idea of experiencing other cultures through food.[2]

Culinary Tourism is the development and promotion of prepared food/drink as an attraction for visitors. Culinary Tourism includes all *unique and memorable* eating and drinking experiences, not just those

---

[2]Lucy M. Long is an Assistant Professor of Popular Culture and Folklore at Bowling Green State University, Bowling Green, Ohio, USA, specializing in folklore, popular culture and ethnomusicology. She is the current editor of *Digest: A Review for the Interdisciplinary Study of Food,* and producer of a documentary video titled *Grand Rapids Apple Butter Festival: Constructing Local Heritage,* funded by the Ohio Humanities Council. Lucy has authored many articles on foodways and ethnomusicology, including: "Culinary Tourism: A Folkloristic Perspective on Eating and Otherness" (contributor and editor, *Southern Folklore Quarterly* 1998); "Holiday Meals: Rituals of Family Tradition" (In *The Meal,* ed. Herbert Meisselman, Aspen Publishers 2000); and "Appalachian Dulcimer," "Hicks Family" (Encyclopedia of Appalachia, forthcoming 2001).
Source: http://www.cohums. ohio-state.edu/cfs/activities/heritage/ biographies.html

Dining al fresco in downtown Vancouver, BC, Canada. Courtesy of Tourism Vancouver

that have earned at least four stars or a favorable review from a journalist. The true Culinary Tourist is not a snob, but rather an explorer who also happens to be an impassioned aficionado of food and drink. Price is not necessarily indicative of quality. For example, visiting a British pub or French cheesemaker are quintessential British and French experiences, although there may not be anything particularly elegant about the visit. True Culinary Tourists are perfectly happy at a roadside café in the middle of nowhere, as long as there is something positively memorable about their dining experience.

destination restaurant
A restaurant that is so interesting, different or special that people travel just to eat there. In other words, the restaurant is their primary destination, not the city or location where the restaurant is found.

Many who attempt to define Culinary Tourism immediately think only of wineries and fine restaurants. Although these are two components of the niche, they are by no means a definitive and final list. Culinary Tourism can happen at a roadside stand (if prepared food is present), or even in the faraway home of a friend you are visiting.

Examples of Culinary Tourism

A few examples will help to illustrate authentic Culinary Tourism experiences. Culinary Tourists travel to:

- See the chef/owner of a noted restaurant make a guest appearance, or even a nightly performance
- See chefs compete
- Eat/drink at, or attend the grand opening of, or special event at, a new or famous restaurant or bar
- Eat/drink at a hard-to-find "locals-only" restaurant or bar
- Participate in a food, wine or beer special event/festival
- Search for unique raw ingredients (e.g., at a grocery, farmers' market, bazaar, or possibly "u-pick" farms for herbs, fruits and vegetables)
- Drive a wine route
- Attend cooking classes (e.g., for a few days, weeks or months)

Culinary Tourism is not limited to individual travelers (FITs) or small groups. Chefs and other professionals can also be Culinary Tourists, especially when they travel to learn about, for example, responsible agricultural practices, or to augment their skills by studying new culinary techniques.

Culinary Tourism is clearly rooted in agriculture. Raw ingredients for the culinary arts come from the air, sea and land. Ingredients such as ripe fruits and vegetables, or fresh meats and fish, are inherently part of the culinary experience. The way chefs prepare the raw ingredients creates culinary art, as well as the unique and memorable Culinary Tourist experience.

Wine tasting in the gorgeous new tasting room of King Estate, one of the largest wineries in Oregon.

Origins of Culinary Tourism

DEEP ROOTS IN AGRICULTURE

Culinary Tourism tends to be inherently more urban than agricultural tourism. The more populated the area, the greater concentration of restaurants, cafés, cooking schools and customers. In addition, high population areas suggest a greater incidence of celebrity chefs, and a propensity for culinary experimentation, as in fusion cooking. In short, one generally finds more culinary "art" in urban areas, even though Culinary Tourism also exists in rural areas, especially in wine-producing regions.

On the macro level, Culinary Tourism is a subset of *cultural tourism*, because cuisine is a manifestation of culture (see figure 1, page 6). Agri-cultural tourism, defined as a subset of rural tourism by the Travel Indus-try Association of America (TIA), includes activities such as visits to farms

© JupiterImages Corporation

What is Culinary Tourism?

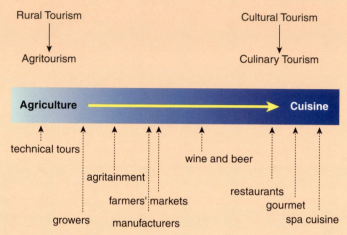

Rural Tourism → Agritourism

Cultural Tourism → Culinary Tourism

Agriculture → Cuisine

technical tours
agritainment
farmers' markets
wine and beer
restaurants
gourmet
spa cuisine
growers
manufacturers

Figure 1 The seeds of culinary tourism are in agriculture, yet culinary tourism is actually a subset of cultural tourism.

and farmers' markets, "u-pick" fruit orchards, ranch stays and agritainment (e.g., pizza "farms" where children learn where the ingredients for a pizza come from). Agritourism focuses more on the technology and process of farming, whereas Culinary Tourism focuses more on prepared food and drink. Obviously there is a degree of cross-over. As there is limited opportunity for a long-term sustainable agricultural industry in heavily urban areas, most agricultural tourism remains inherently rural.

A major difference exists between Culinary Tourism in urban and rural settings. For example, the population of rural towns swells severalfold every weekend, when tourists from larger cities descend upon them. Smaller towns have a much more difficult time integrating large numbers of tourists than do larger cities. The environmental impact of culinary tourists on small towns vs. large cities is a topic needing further research.

Food prepared in the countryside tends to be fresher than that delivered to restaurants in larger cities. However, that statement is arguable, as good chefs source their ingredients from countless suppliers. In U.S. cities such as Portland, Oregon, where one can be on a farm in the countryside literally within a 30 minute drive from downtown, it is not unreasonable that local chefs can have access to the absolute highest quality seasonal ingredients every day. Yet it is reasonable to assume that chefs in larger cities may have better access to unique and hard-to-find ingredients than do rural chefs.

GREEN CHEFS AND THE CHEF'S COLLABORATIVE

Respect for the farmers' way of life and responsible agricultural cultivation is the tenet echoed by "green" chefs around the world. Chef Greg Higgins of Higgins Restaurant in Portland, Oregon, and Alice Waters of Chez Panisse in Berkeley, California (both U.S. cities), are two of the strongest proponents of this movement. These "green" chefs tout the advantages of adopting a holistic "farm to table" approach to restaurant management. The hard work of these two individuals has helped to take restaurateurs' agricultural responsibility to a historically significant level. Chefs with similar mindsets have come together to create an organization called the Chef's Collaborative.

The Chef's Collaborative, a network of North America's most influential and well-known chefs, continues to add members on a regular basis, and attrition is low. Founded in 1993 by chefs as an educational initiative, "the Collaborative is committed to developing educational programs for children, to strengthening farmer/chef connections, and to providing good, safe and wholesome food by emphasizing locally-grown seasonally fresh, and whole or minimally processed food in their restaurants."[3] This movement is particularly evident in the Pacific Northwest of the United States and Canada.

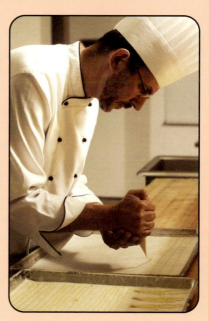

© 2006 JupiterImages Corporation

This "back to the roots" approach has filtered down to restaurant patrons as well. One regularly overhears customers inquiring whether ingredients are organic, free range, cruelty free, raised locally or imported, GMO-free, seasonal and so on. The catch-all phrase that has evolved to include all of these terms is FLOSS (fresh, local, organic, sustainable and seasonal).[4] The popularity of responsible agricultural practices and the recent surge in usage of ingredients farmed in this manner portends future culinary innovation, which will help to fuel Culinary Tourism.

---

[3] http://www.chefscollaborative.org
[4] Term coined by Stephan Earnhart, Director of Operations, Ritz Carlton Members Beach Club, Sarasota, Florida, USA.

Contributors to Culinary Tourism

Contributors to Culinary Tourism come from a number of sources. Many people read the food columns of their local newspapers or popular food magazines such as *Gourmet* or *Australian Gourmet Traveller,* both of which heavily emphasize the intersection of cuisine and travel. Television programming on the Food Network (U.S.) e.g., shows like Rachel Ray's $40 a Day, do their share to pique curiosity in savory delights from faraway lands. In addition to travel shows on the Food Network, the Travel Channel often features segments on local food and drink. Media consumers are taught to seek out culinary adventures when they travel. Cuisine often becomes a hobby, if not a new passion.

PRODUCT SAMPLING AND PRODUCT PLACEMENT

Some Culinary Tourists are born through product sampling. Many of us have been lucky enough to try Biscoff's cookies on a commercial airline flight. According to the maker of these delightful wafers, "[i]n an effort to reach customers who had never tried these wonderful biscuits, we began distributing Biscoff Biscuits on airlines in 1984, to the delight of thousands of passengers. In response to overwhelming demand for the biscuits, a mail order catalogue was developed. In 1999, we launched [our website] and find that we are attracting an even wider group of 'Biscoff Fans' around the world!"[5] In less than 20 years, the manufacturer not only succeeded in building awareness about its product, but cultivated an appreciation for this unique style of caramelized cookie that originated from Belgium. Culinary Tourists are exploratory and will make a point of "discovering" the places where products, such as the caramelized Biscoff cookies, were originally made.

Culture-specific product sampling abounds. On many of its flights, Virgin Atlantic serves a typical English high tea of scones with Devonshire

---

[5]For more information, visit http://www.biscoff.com

In France, all roads lead to Champagne. © 2006 JupiterImages Corporation

cream and jam, along with tea or coffee. United Airlines proudly serves the American Starbucks coffee, recalling the coffee culture mystique that is rooted in the U.S. Pacific Northwest, home of the Starbucks company.

Special guests at historic Timberline Lodge in the U.S. state of Oregon receive a satchel of Chukar Cherries' Mt. Hood Trail Mix, a mélange of dried Oregon cranberries and Oregon hazelnuts, when they arrive in their room.[6] Some hotel guests may also receive a bottle of locally produced wine or H2O, an Oregon mineral water.

Product sampling, especially in the hospitality sector, has educated consumers and raised their curiosity about local food and drink. In doing so, it has helped consumers associate certain food and drink with particular cultures and destinations. Product sampling is pervasive and it appears to contribute significantly to tourists' knowledge of local food and drink. The degree to which product sampling affects tourists' knowledge of local food and drink is a subject worthy of further research.

Product placement can also generate interest in travel. The hit U.K. television series, "Absolutely Fabulous," made Kettle brand potato chips from the U.S. state of Oregon an instant hit in the United Kingdom. Now

[6]For more information, visit http://www.timberline.com and http://www.chukar.com

visitors to the United Kingdom can find these delicious chips for sale the moment they land at London's Heathrow airport, as well as in grocers throughout the country. The Kettle Foods company could do more, however, to build a cachet for, and interest in, its Oregon home, a spectacular destination itself. This culinary tourism marketing partnership has not yet been consummated.

Multicultural societies like the United States and Brazil, as well as international cities like London and Paris, have also raised consumer awareness of different cuisines and ingredients. The evolution of fusion cuisine is an example. For example, Frattini restaurant, located in the Italian Leichardt district of Sydney, New South Wales, Australia, is known as an Italian restaurant. Yet, an occasional Asian spice such as star anise or ginger finds its way into an otherwise typically Italian dish. The resulting flavors and textures are positively unforgettable. Such mixing underscores the ethnic influences in multicultural societies, and plants the seed for future travels to the lands where these flavors originate.

> **fusion cuisine**
> Fusing two or more disparate cuisines to create an interesting dish that would not likely have originated on its own in its parent cultures.

The mixing of cultures, global air travel, the Internet and television have raised consumer awareness, knowledge, sophistication and expectations to extremely high levels. To the surprise and even offense of many waiters, restaurant patrons often know more about the food being served, where it was grown, how it was prepared, and so on, than do the waiters. Chefs, winemakers and brewers are continually challenged to come up with new and exciting products and presentations to assuage the curiosity of increasingly jaded consumers.

Understanding the Culinary Tourist

CULINARY TOURIST PROFILE

While few demographic and psychographic data exist to draw a comprehensive picture of the typical Culinary Tourist, one major study conducted in Canada can help. In March 2001, the Canadian Tourism Commission released "TAMS: Travel Activities & Motivation Survey, Wine & Cuisine Report," one of the most comprehensive profiles available of Culinary Tourists. According to the report, both "young and mature singles as well as young and mature couples were the most likely to exhibit an interest in vacation activities associated with wine and cuisine. Interest in such activities also increased as the level of education and household income increased."[7] While these data represented Canadian travelers, the results for U.S. travelers were extremely similar. The report did not break travelers down by specific age groups, but rather categorized travelers as "young" or "mature."

The report found a high correlation between Culinary Tourists and exploration. In other words, Culinary Tourists are explorers. "Those who exhibit an interest in vacation activities associated with wine and cuisine were considerably more likely to have *sought out* vacation experiences associated with exploration (e.g. visiting historical sites, natural wonders), personal indulgences (e.g. to experience the good life, visiting a casino, experiencing city life such as night life) and romance and relaxation (e.g. to experience intimacy and romance,

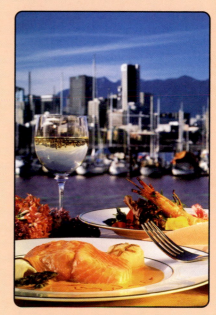

Courtesy of Tourism Vancouver

---

[7]"Travel Activities & Motivation Survey (TAMS), Wine & Cuisine Report." Lang Research. March 2001. p. 6.

relax and recuperate.)"[8] As the report evaluated the demographic behavior of Canadian and American Culinary Tourists, an opportunity exists to investigate whether Culinary Tourists from other countries share similar demographic and psychographic traits.

CULINARY TOURISTS ARE EXPLORERS

Many people, especially foodservice managers and chefs, have had a hard time defining and grasping Culinary Tourism. What does it mean to travel for the sake of eating and drinking? The TAMS report suggests that a large element of culinary travel is exploration as tourists search for new restaurants, new ingredients and different artistic presentations. It has been said that the "very best winery to visit is the one you find yourself, like that Italian restaurant around the corner that only you know about."[9]

Travel industry professionals recognize niche markets such as bird watching and youth sports, which are clearly defined. Until recently, Culinary Tourism was usually and understandably overlooked. Did the diner find his way to the restaurant because he was hungry, because he had heard about it and wanted to try it or because of chance? There is little research to explain what motivates diners or Culinary Tourists, although the body of knowledge is growing.

CULINARY TOURISM IS EXPERIENTIAL AND INTERACTIVE

Aging baby boomers show an affinity for hands-on or experiential tourism.[10] The act of eating or drinking fulfills their desire for a hands-on, interactive experience. Dining is a form of interactive theater, as the interaction with the waiter serves as a kind of show or entertainment for the diners. Furthermore, experiences that involve the five senses will be more memorable than those that do not. Culinary art is the only form of art that involves each of the five senses: Diners *see* their food, *smell* its aroma, *feel* the textures, *hear* the chewing, and *taste* the flavors. Since the experience of eating and drinking involves all five human senses (smell, sight, sound, taste, touch), visitors are more likely to remember their dining experience far longer than most other vacation/holiday experiences.

---

[8]TAMS, p. 14.
[9]Gaiter, Dorothy J. and John Brecher, "Beating the Crush," *Wall Street Journal,* July 12, 2002, p. W6.
[10]"The Marketing Decade: Setting the Australian Wine Marketing Agenda 2000 >> 2010," Winemakers' Federation of Australia and Australian Wine and Brandy Corporation, p. 16.

MOVERS AND SHAKERS

The Australian Tourist Commission (ATC) was one of the first destination marketing organizations (DMOs) to make a commitment to Culinary Tourism. Creativity, staff, money and a challenging remote location at the corner of the globe have all contributed to molding the ATC into one of the world's leading destination marketing organizations. Its strategic planners and marketers are among the world's best. In addition to the brief questionnaires found on the back of the Australian immigration forms that visitors receive upon arrival in the country, the ATC conducts other research on a regular basis. Its extensive market research fuels the development of solid marketing and product development strategies. According to a formal press release issued by the ATC in March 2000, "Tourism statistics showed experiencing Australian food and visiting wine regions were two of the top five factors influencing international visitors' decision to come to Australia."[11] Since then, regional DMOs in Australia have begun to take the ATC's lead and are developing their own regional Culinary Tourism strategies.

© 2006 JupiterImages Corporation

---

[11]http://atc.australia.com/newscenter.asp?art=294

The Canadians have also demonstrated a similar level of commitment to Culinary Tourism. In March 2001, the Canadian Tourist Commission received the results from the previously mentioned TAMS, a major research project on the behavioral motivation of food and wine tourists.[12] The results showed that Culinary Tourists were high spenders and enjoyed cultural activities such as theater, music festivals and shopping, as well as outdoor recreation such as golf, skiing and rafting, in addition to their pursuit of noteworthy local food and drink experiences. This report led first to a Culinary Tourism strategy for the province of Ontario, and then a national Culinary Tourism development strategy.[13] The TAMS report is due to be updated in 2006 and will provide a welcome addition to the body of available Culinary Tourism knowledge.

In July 2003, Nestle South Africa acknowledged the "global thinking that food tourism is increasingly becoming an important niche market, [and] initiated a project to develop and promote South African cuisine within the theme of 'Local is Lekker to World Renown."[14] Lekker is the Afrikaans and Dutch word for "attractive" or "tasty." A combination of South African wines, fresh seafood and a crossroads of multiple cultures has set the stage for South Africa to emerge as a serious player at the international Culinary Tourism table.

Other destinations, such as France's Burgundy region or Italy's Tuscany, have been culinary leaders for hundreds of years. Only recently have tourists been able to travel there in large numbers, especially for culinary reasons, perhaps to see how truffles are foraged, or to learn regional Italian cooking techniques. While cuisine is an integral part of the tourist experience in France and Italy, DMOs in those countries have largely *not* focused on strategies to develop, refine and capitalize on interest in gastronomy. A destination resting on its former culinary laurels provides the precursor to its culinary demise. Consider the state of the French wine industry, which has lost enormous market share to Chile, Argentina, South Africa and Australia. Or consider the restaurant scene in San Francisco, which was once widely regarded as the restaurant capital of the United States. Much to the surprise of many San Francisco residents, laziness, arrogance, or both have unseated San Francisco's restaurants from the city's num-

---

[12]It appears that the research was commissioned in April 2000 and results were published in March 2001. For more information, see Bibliography.

[13]"Acquiring a Taste for Cuisine Tourism: A Product Development Strategy," Canadian Tourism Commission, Ottawa, Ontario, Canada. June 2002.

[14]http://www.winenews.co.za

ber one position in the United States in favor of newer, nimbler and more eager restaurants in destinations such as Portland, Oregon; Santa Fe, New Mexico; Memphis, Tennessee and of course powerhouse Las Vegas, Nevada.

Several noteworthy destinations demonstrate leadership or leadership potential in the Culinary Tourism niche, including New York City; Las Vegas; New Orleans; Miami; Brazil; New Zealand; Sydney and Melbourne, Australia; Western Australia; Spain; Greece; Singapore; Shanghai, China; Bali, Indonesia; Japan; Canada; South Africa and many, many more.

Sydney Harbour Bridge © 2006 JupiterImages Corporation

Culinary Tourism's Economic Potential

DATA SCARCE BUT INSIGHTFUL

Data on Culinary Tourism is hard to come by. The more that cuisine is accepted as a mainstream attraction by destination marketers, the more research that will be done to further develop and justify the niche.

It may seem obvious, but consider that 100 percent of tourists dine out when traveling.[15] Data show that tourists, some of whom have expense accounts, enjoy dining out. These data also show that dining is the most popular activity after tourists arrive at a new destination.[16] Data also show that the higher the total dinner bill, the more likely those patrons are tourists.[17] This suggests that people are more willing, or perhaps more able, to spend money eating out while traveling than they would in their place of residence.

Tourists who like to eat well cannot spend all of their time dining and drinking. There is a high correlation between tourists interested in wine/cuisine and those interested in visiting museums, theater, shopping, music/film festivals and participating in outdoor recreation.[18] Interest in Culinary Tourism spans all age groups, and the size of the potential market is large.[19]

LUCRATIVE, SUSTAINABLE DEVELOPMENT

Culinary Tourism can be profitable. Napa Valley, California, USA, is a case in point. According to the Napa and Sonoma Valley visitor associations, 10 million visitors per year spend USD 2 billion in the two

---

[15]The point is noted that conventioneers, for whom meals are often entirely provided, may not necessarily have the opportunity to experience true local cuisine. Additionally, visitors dining in the home of a friend or relative are not "dining out" in a foodservice setting, but they may still experience a cuisine different from what they would normally eat at home.
[16]http://www.restaurant.org/tourism/facts.cfm
[17]Ibid.
[18]"TAMS: Travel Activities & Motivation Survey, Wine & Cuisine Report," Lang Research, on behalf of Canadian Tourism Commission, March 2001, p. 16.
[19]Ibid.

counties.[20] This equates to an expenditure of USD 200 per visitor per year.[21] According to the Napa Valley Conference & Visitors Bureau, day visitors spend an average of USD 150 per day and overnight visitors spend an average of USD 300 per day. Room rates in Napa Valley average USD 150 per night (the average length of stay in the area is 2.9 days).

Given the data for Napa/Sonoma, 10,000,000 visitors per year x USD 200 per visitor = USD 2 billion of *direct* economic impact.[22] The economic impact is visibly evident in the well-maintained buildings and roads. There is clearly considerable opportunity, at least in Napa/Sonoma, to develop group packages and encourage visitors to stay longer and spend more money in the area. Rather than day trips out of San Francisco, which account for the vast majority of visits to Napa/Sonoma, a greater emphasis on encouraging visitors to stay overnight longer and/or to view Napa/Sonoma as their primary, not secondary, destination would increase the overall revenue and tax collections. The message to hoteliers and hotel developers is that there is an opportunity to develop more affordable and quality lodging options in culinary areas where good lodging is scarce or prohibitively expensive.

Similar economic impact is reported in the Australian state of Tasmania, a well-known wine-producing region. There, in 2000, visitors spent an average of AUD 1489 (USD 1113) per trip, and AUD 146 (USD 109) per night.[23,24] Generally the "direct economic impact of wine tourism in Australia is estimated at between AUD $400–500 million (USD 299–373 million) per year, primarily comprised of direct wine sales at wineries."[25]

These figures do not factor in the considerable amount spent on food and wine purchases that are taken back home. According to Tourism Tasmania, in 2000, 76.5 percent of visitors to Tasmania purchased wine, with an average expenditure of AUD 113 (USD 84) per person.[26] If a large number of visitors originate from another country, then it stands to reason that a strong Culinary Tourism industry could

---

[20]Gaiter, p. W6.

[21]Sources: Napa Valley Visitor Profile; http://www.napachamber.org/tourism_demographics.html; and http://www.napachamber.org/ag_and_wines.html.

[22]Figures on indirect economic impact are not available.

[23]Tourism Tasmania, "Wine Survey 2000, Chart: Expenditure of Tasmanian Wineries," no page.

[24]Rate of exchange (ROE): 1 USD = 1.33823 AUD, Jan. 5, 2006. Source: http:///www.xe.net.

[25]"Strategy for Wine & Culinary Tourism in Ontario: Background Report, Section: Australia—An Emerging Wine Tourism Destination," March 2001, p. 62.

[26]Tourism Tasmania, no page.

favorably impact the balance of trade. More research is needed on the economic impact of Culinary Tourism on foreign trade.

Additional examples of the economic impact of Culinary Tourism are scarce, but the message is clear. Culinary Tourism is potentially a very lucrative niche that holds strong potential for economic and community development, as shown in Figure 2 below. Tourism based around food and drink helps support the livelihoods of local agricultural producers and promotes the maintenance of high quality and purity in food and drink. When tourists fill otherwise empty restaurant tables, more sales are made. More sales mean more profit and more capital to reinvest in the community. The local tax base benefits as well. Culinary Tourism can make significant contributions toward sustainable community and economic development.

Consider the African-American community in the U.S. city of San Francisco. The 59 African-American-owned restaurants in San Francisco formed a cooperative in September 2005 to build brand identity and promote traffic. According to John Templeton of the African-American Tourism Council in San Francisco, the establishments attract thousands of customers monthly and employ close to 500 workers. The restaurants are sponsoring an amendment to the city's small and local business enterprise ordinance to encourage further city contracting with businesses that provide employment anchors in emerging neighborhoods. More jobs mean fewer idle people and less trouble on the street, a solid step toward the area's sustainable economic and community development.

The chart shows the interconnection between food/beverage and tourism in a community's economic development. Tourists and locals spend money on food and beverage. Their spending adds to the local government's tax base, part of which is spent on community infrastructure and service development. Business owners make profits and then spend at least some of those profits back in the local community.

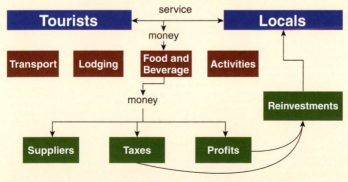

Figure 2   Role of food/beverage in the tourism industry.

Benefits of Culinary Tourism For Foodservice

Culinary Tourism is a different and potentially valuable product to add to a destination's product mix. Like other tourists, Culinary Tourists leave their money and return home. Strain on the infrastructure is temporary and generally minimal, unless the destination experiences unsustainable popularity and growth, such as is the case in California's Napa Valley, where serious weekend traffic jams, long lines in restaurants and prohibitively expensive hotel room rates are guaranteed.

Culinary Tourism still benefits local farmers, yet the focus is on the direct and immediate benefit to the consumer or traveler, rather than to the farmer, an important point in positioning Culinary Tourism products for sale.

Culinary Tourism also fosters inter-regional and intra-regional competition, which has its positive and negative points. For example, Australia and New Zealand compete for the same long-haul Culinary Tourists. Due to the long-haul nature of flights to those countries from most of the world, Culinary Tourists are likely to choose one destination over another. The same is the case for France and Italy, with two very different culinary experiences. Yet in other regions such as the U.S. Pacific Northwest and Canada, regional competition and the synergy of complementary products help to raise the overall quality of the visitor's

> **carrying capacity**
> The maximum number of tourists that a destination can absorb before the infrastructure is strained and services begin to suffer (this can be represented by the top of a bell curve before the slope starts to descend). For example, the consistently large number of tourists in California's Napa Valley means that the destination exceeds its carrying capacity on a regular basis. Research is needed to determine which resources, businesses, policies or other solutions are needed to bring the visitor impact back below the destination's carrying capacity.

© 2006 JupiterImages Corporation

experience and the products offered. The competition and synergy work together to promote intra-regional tourism in this example. Specifically for foodservice providers, Culinary Tourism:

- Provides more sales, more profits, more capital to reinvest
- Puts non-central businesses "on the map"
- Offers cooperative marketing opportunities for more potential impact than businesses can afford individually (smaller and local businesses share equal ground with larger ones)
- Participates at ground level of new niche opportunities, ability to capitalize on a trend
- Helps raise quality of nearby business products and services
- Fosters additional business opportunities: cellar door sales, customized wine labels, product shipping centers, additional restaurants

Addtional Benefits of Culinary Tourism

Benefits for Travel Industry

- Helps fill hotel rooms and restaurant tables that otherwise remain empty
- Creates new DMO memberships from "hidden" businesses
- Takes advantage of post-September 11 (2001) trends toward local/regional tourism
- Offers a new, largely unexplored market; with significant development potential
- Provides positive, differentiating selling point for convention/meeting business and tour operators
- Fosters additional business partnership opportunities: lodging, B&Bs, attractions

Benefits for Residents and Communities

- Creates additional jobs, many in suburban and rural areas
- Helps residents to see and understand the economic impact of tourism
- Promotes cross-cultural awareness and understanding
- Offers greater economic prosperity
- Grows tax base
- Benefits neighboring/en route communities through overflow and transient business
- Helps unify disjointed communities
- Fosters additional business opportunities: support services

Benefits for Tourists

- Offers access to unique products (e.g., wines, beers, foods) that are not available beyond the establishment's doors
- Provides exclusive product sampling, purchase offers and club memberships

© 2006 JupiterImages Corporation

- Tourists enjoy higher quality (food, ambiance) due to higher standards and greater competition than in non-culinary areas
- Creates allure of being a trend-setter and participating in a cutting-edge niche, resulting in "bragging rights"

Benefits for Manufacturers and Exporters
- more product samples mean more samples brought home to share or brag about and more requests for product imports
- additional business opportunities: retail/cellar door sales, customized wine labels, product shipping centers, additional restaurants

Benefits for Governments
- increased tax base from increased sales
- additional jobs, many in suburban and rural areas
- tourism investment does not require new infrastructure
- neighboring/en route communities benefit from overflow and transient business

Benefits for Visitors

- access to unique products (e.g. wines, beers, foods) that are not available beyond establishment's doors)
- exclusive product sampling, purchase offers and club memberships
- enjoy higher quality (food, ambiance) due to higher standards and greater competition than in non-culinary areas
- allure of being a trend-setter and participating in a cutting-edge niche—bestows "bragging rights"

Designing a Culinary Tourism Product Strategy

Developing marketable and salable culinary products is the first step to capitalizing on the mushrooming Culinary Tourism industry. For example, it is amazing to see the number of destinations that choose to promote their local farmers' market as a visitor attraction. Consider the fact that there is little visitors can do with fresh rhubarb (unless they are staying at a friend's house and have access to a kitchen) and the fallacy of this marketing becomes clear. These types of markets exist all around the world and unless they are famous for a particular reason (San Francisco's Ferry

© 2006 JupiterImages Corporation

Terminal Building Market) or especially well-developed (Seattle's Pike Place Market), a market alone is not a compelling reason to draw huge numbers of visitors from beyond a day drive radius. Likewise, destinations that depend on an overnight room tax as a source of revenue will be disappointed with the room tax return on investment of farmers' market promotions. Yet a few destinations do offer unique and memorable farmers' market experiences. The farmers' market in the beautiful and historic San Francisco Ferry Terminal Building is the classic example.

Additionally, many agricultural products cannot be transported across (U.S.) state lines or exported from one country to another for health and disease reasons. Therefore, it becomes critical for Culinary Tourists to enjoy local cheeses and meats in situ.

Similarly, food and beverage events can either generate room nights or keep tourists at bay, depending on how they are positioned. For example, the Gilroy Garlic Festival in California offers more booths featuring art of questionable value than it does food, let alone food featuring garlic. Visitors traveling to this festival from great distances will be terribly disappointed in this type of experience that many would call a "tourist trap." The 2005 Taste of Chicago event, however, saw 3.64 million visitors and generated just over USD 100 million—no small change for any business. The event, attended by both locals and visitors, is large and exciting enough to give visitors a reason to drive (or fly) to Chicago for a long weekend, which generates overnight room business as well. Food and beverage events of a smaller magnitude, such as most local festivals created around local agricultural products, are typically of interest to the local area, but again, offer little promise to attract overnight visitors unless value-added products (gifts of high perceived value available only to package-buyers, themed dinners featuring the agricultural product in every course, and so on) are packaged with the festival or event, or the festival product theme is inherently unique or rare (such as truffles). *Food festivals and events are not an economic panacea,* although many businesses and destination marketing organizations approach them as if they are.

Still other Culinary Tourism products can be created to revolve around food preparation and training. Consider chef demos, or in-the-kitchen chef training. Such activities are relatively easy to assemble, but the components must deliver on the promise of quality; otherwise, the intended effect of customer satisfaction may backfire. Successful programs will typically feature a noted chef (who perhaps published a cookbook), noteworthy ingredients (either locally grown/manufactured or of unique or rare status), or take place in a

celebrity chef
A chef who has achieved notoriety. Examples include Julia Child, Emeril and David Boulet.

unique and memorable venue (historic building such as a castle or old house; charming pastoral farm, and so on). Even simply sitting at the chef's table (or in front of the kitchen) in a restaurant can provide the kind of "dinner with a show" experience that satisfies Culinary Tourists.

Food factory tours are often presented to visitors with the expectation that all will walk away not just satisfied, but with purchases in hand. However, factory tours are increasingly difficult to offer due to health and food safety risks. Many of the more prestigious food manufacturers are smaller gourmet or "boutique" producers that started small and still do not have sufficient space or visitor-friendly facilities to host tours. Other manufacturers, such as Kellogg's cereals, will not offer tours, purportedly for reasons of corporate espionage.

boutique chef

Derived from "boutique hotel," a term that refers to a small, fashionable hotel property with specialized service. A "boutique chef" is a chef with a noteworthy and memorable personal style that sets him or her apart from other chefs and restaurants. The chef may do this by using ingredients of exceptional quality or which are truly unique. The chef can also set him/herself apart by preparing combinations of flavors or textures that are truly unforgettable, and by preparing the finished dish as a work of art.

Venues for Culinary Tourism

Culinary Tourism happens in various venues. The most obvious such venues are cafés, bars, and restaurants where eating and drinking take place. Culinary Tourists are apt to visit unique, local restaurants, but tend to shy away from chain restaurants, which have typically offered diners little hope for positive culinary memories. However, that is now changing as well. *USA Today* recently reported how quick service (formerly "fast food") restaurants are now upgrading their menus to meet the demands of discriminating consumers. Now, instead of a grilled chicken sandwich, we find "Foster Farms® Grilled Chicken on Rosemary Ciabatta with Pesto Mayonnaise and Arugula".

Not every meal can be a memory, and there is still an important place for the world's quick service restaurants to serve Culinary Tourists. For example, in the U.S. state of Oregon, local Tillamook Cheese partners with McDonald's to use its cheese on the Big n Tasty hamburger. Burgerville, a competing local quick service restaurant, partners with Oregon's Rogue Creamery to feature its world-award winning Rogue Blue Cheese on its Bacon Blue Cheeseburgers.

In wineries, food is sometimes available in addition to the wine (e.g., at an adjoining café or at a winemaker's dinner). Wineries are relatively easy to find, especially if they are on a dedicated wine route that makes discovery and sampling easy for Culinary Tourists. Wineries, and many farms, often have gift shops that promote other local prepared foods as well.

Breweries and distilleries each contribute their share to the Culinary Tourism phenomenon. Consider the many wonderful U.K. ales, Scottish whiskey or German pilsners that quench the thirst of many an urban hiker. Portland, Oregon, with its 32 microbreweries, has more breweries than any other city in the world. Oregon is renowned for its microbrew beers, which have won several international medals, including the prestigious Brewing Industry International Awards in London, United Kingdom. Awards and the corresponding media coverage add to consumer

wine and food pairing

Choosing a specific wine that is best suited to accompany a particular food. For example, most people prefer to drink specific red wines with meat and white wines with fish. A sommelier, or wine steward, takes the pairing a step further and chooses particular vineyards and vintages that s/he feels would best suit the food in question.

CHAPTER 10 • Venues for Culinary Tourism

© 2006 JupiterImages Corporation

curiosity, and contribute to the desire to travel and see where the magic is made.

An interpretive center along a wine route or at a brewery explains to visitors something about the manufacturing process, and possibly about the nature of the product or local agriculture as well. A notable arrival in the world of culinary interpretive centers is COPIA: American Centre for Wine, Food & the Arts, located in California's Napa Valley. The idea was born of legendary vintner Robert Mondavi, who wanted to create an institution to celebrate American achievements in the culinary and winemaking arts. An expensive USD 60 million project, COPIA's profitability and success remain to be seen.

In 2001, another notable example, the National Wine Centre of Australia, opened in Adelaide, South Australia. The National Wine Centre serves to educate visitors about, and also promote, Australian wines.[27] It also serves as a shipping center, making it effortless for visitors to buy and ship home their wine purchases, thereby helping Australia's trade balance. Wine regions in other countries could learn from Australia's National Wine Centre. While it is rumored that the Australian Wine Centre has had a rough time for various reasons, it remains an interesting example and one worthy of further study.

Events are another popular way to promote Culinary Tourism. For example, celebrity chefs may agree to make an appearance for a charity event such as Taste of the Nation, which is an event produced by Share Our Strength, an international nonprofit hunger relief organization headquartered in Washington, DC, USA.[28] A series of 75 events takes place for one night in each of 75 host cities across North America. Some cities have multiple events on multiple days. Chefs from some of the most prestigious restaurants wine and dine partygoers, all to benefit various hunger relief organizations. The events raise millions of dollars each year and participating restaurants benefit from several million dollars worth of free media coverage.

While culinary events can be fun, top chefs have limited time and cannot appear at all of the events that request their presence. Events are

---

[27]For more information, visit http://www.wineaustralia.com.au
[28]For more information, visit http://www.strength.org/taste

Courtesy of Tourism Vancouver

also expensive to produce and generally require a time investment of at least 3 years before they are profitable. American Express is the major underwriter of Taste of the Nation. Other sponsors include illy coffee, Evian water, Coors beer, Tyson foods and many others. The corporate partner will require a solid, measurable return on investment. Destinations with limited funding, and which seek to develop this market, are advised to partner with respectful, partnership-oriented corporations to secure the required financial support.

Event timing is crucial. Destinations with multiple events would do well to publish an event matrix for businesses to avoid conflicts and leverage economies of scale by grouping or combining similar events. Based on the matrix, the DMO can then publish a calendar of events for use by both consumers and the media. Events also tend to be poorly publicized, usually only on local or regional levels. Limited promotion precludes higher-spending international visitors from integrating all but the largest, most prominent events into their vacation/holiday plans.

The publicity timetable is just as crucial to successful food and beverage event marketing. Many magazines publish their editorial calendar a full year or more in advance. Event calendars are often finalized as many as four months before an actual event date. Event promoters who mail a press release or timid e-mail request two weeks before the event date may be baffled why their notices fall on deaf ears. Planning is everything.

Events do not have to be as chic as Taste of the Nation to attract Culinary Tourists. Becky Mecuri, author of *Food Festival U.S.A.*, states that "visiting local food festivals is the best way to get a sense of a community's flavor."[29] The local DMO can organize a simple chili cook-off contest and promote it 100 miles/160 km in all directions. Such an event very much qualifies as Culinary Tourism if it brings visitors from outside the immediate local area (typically regarded as 50 miles/80 km).

Local festivals often have a theme. Ethnic themes are popular, such as the St. Gregory's Armenian Festival in Chicago, Illinois, USA, which takes place every August. Food-specific themes, such as the Garlic Festival in Gilroy, California, USA, and the Elephant Garlic Festival in North Plains, Oregon, USA, are also popular.

Sometimes events will advertize guest speakers, such as a chef of world-renown like Alice Waters or David Boulet, or someone of lesser notoriety like a local winemaker who discusses how and why her wines compare favorably to France's red burgundies.

Summer al fresco dining

Local farmers' markets are regular events that take place during the growing months. While generally featuring fruits, vegetables, flowers and sometimes meats, farmers' markets are at first glance of more interest to *agricultural* tourists. Yet more and more farmers' markets now feature prepared foods, such as pies and other baked goods, artisan cheeses and breads, and even ethnic foods. Other markets, such as the one found in the San Francisco Ferry Terminal Building, are geared entirely to an upscale consumer experience, although fresh produce is often available outside. Culinary Tourists will likely keep themselves busy for quite a while at such markets.

Festivals, events and markets are excellent ways for smaller producers to distribute and promote their product. When visitors sample the local products at such venues and discuss the products they like with their

[29] *The Oregonian*, July 9, 2002, p. FD4.

friends, a "buzz" or "word-of-mouth" ensues. Word of mouth is one of the most effective and least expensive kinds of promotion. Such "hype" is also what the media seeks to focus on and/or helps to promote, when they report on new products or new destinations.

While events are a popular way to attract tourists and locals alike, the success of many food/beverage events is not well documented, and often the economic impact is not well tracked. Blame it on well-intentioned volunteers or inexperienced event producers; regardless, the end result is the same: Institutional memory is lost by not documenting the event's success on an annual basis. More research is needed on the economic impact of food/beverage events on local communities.

Culinary Tourism can also take the shape of education. A few companies offer organized tours dedicated to agritourism, and still fewer focus on culinary tours of a region. In between meals, such companies must balance culinary offerings with interesting activities, such as theater, museums or outdoor activities. Destinations that offer a balanced and compelling value proposition to Culinary Tourists are most likely to succeed in building a strong tourism base.

More frequently, Culinary Tourism may be experienced as a component of a mainstream tour, such as a small, organized ski tour to the Swiss Alps, where every night after a long day on the slopes the group enjoys hearty Swiss cooking and elusive but wonderful Swiss wines. Such visitors may never even consider themselves Culinary Tourists, yet they very much are.

The educational component of Culinary Tourism is evident in another way. The advent of easily accessible and affordable international travel, combined with the surge in popularity of cooking television shows, has given rise to an interest in attending cooking schools and even hospitality management programs abroad. It is not unusual to hear of someone who goes to France for two weeks for an intensive pastry class, or to Italy for eight weeks for an in-depth overview of Italian culinary techniques. Le Cordon Bleu schools, for example, frequently woo students from other countries. Visitors must stay in lodging and invariably spend other money while they are residents for an extended period of time. Many young people enroll in two-year programs at culinary academies around the world. They are short-term residents, or long-term tourists, still spending money to support the local economy.

The destinations with the best chance of developing a Culinary Tourism product are those that already have the advantageous "ingredients" to support a Culinary Tourism strategy. Such resources include creative chefs, wineries, proximity to a rich agricultural area, unique agricultural products, and so on. Nevertheless, Culinary Tourism thrives in agriculture-poor destinations such as Las Vegas, which succeeds due to a number of unique circumstances that include a wealth of existing entertainment, global notoriety and a proactive and well-funded destination marketing organization.

Culinary Tourism is the primary tourism product in only a handful of destinations. Most destinations offer another solid core product, into which Culinary Tourism integrates. For example, Aspen, Colorado, USA, and Whistler, British Columbia, Canada, offer visitors the same core product—winter sports. A wealthier demographic among winter sports enthusiasts, as well as international name recognition, helped each destination to develop a credible Culinary Tourism product. Given Whistler's location near the abundant, rich agricultural areas of British Columbia (seas rich with fish, forests rich with game, orchards full of fruits, and a burgeoning wine industry), Whistler arguably has a greater number of resources at its immediate disposal than does Aspen, making it a destination with greater culinary potential and appeal. It is interesting to note that Aspen's Food & Wine Classic takes place in June, a low season when room nights are desperately needed and local agricultural resources are more readily available. Colorado does produce some excellent wines, must to the surprise of almost every wine drinker. Recent rumors indicate that Colorado's wine industry, which hails from the far western Grand Junction area of the state (a couple of hours' drive west of the ski areas), is interested in partnering with Colorado's ski resorts for product sampling opportunities, a wise move if they are to gain the national and international recognition their wines very much deserve.

Destinations serious about developing their Culinary Tourism product should first perform an asset inventory: What are your destination's unique culinary assets? Does your area produce a unique food item? Does a certain kind of fruit grow only where you live? Is a specific culinary technique indigenous to your area? This inventory is then sorted according to resource (restaurant, café, manufacturer, winery, grocery, and so on). Determine how many resources exist in each category. An informal ranking process helps to identify which assets are worthy of further refinement and promotion in the marketplace. The Association offers more information at http://www.culinarytourism.org.

In 2002, the Canadian Tourism Commission published "Acquiring a Taste for Cuisine Tourism: A Product Development Strategy." This work, an example of a destination that has taken a serious look at addressing these kinds of product development and marketing issues,[30] is

---

[30]"Acquiring a Taste for Cuisine Tourism: A Product Development Strategy," Canadian Tourism Commission, Ottawa, Ontario, Canada, June 2002.

an excellent road map for the development of Canada's Culinary Tourism product and may have relevance for other destinations too.

What are your destination's strengths? Weaknesses? What exists in the market that could be an opportunity of threat? What kinds of partnerships could you forge to take your Culinary Tourism product development to the next level? An asset inventory is one part of the Culinary Tourism Summit, which is a component of the International Culinary Tourism Association's Education Program.

Visit http://www.culinarytourism.org/education for more information about organizing a summit in your area.

Caveats of Culinary Tourism

SERVICE

The quality of service makes a significant contribution to the potential success or failure of Culinary Tourism. Service quality has always been an issue in the hospitality business, especially in cultures where service to guests is held in high esteem, notably Asia and parts of Europe. Like other tourists, Culinary Tourists will be disappointed by any number of adverse dining experiences, including lack of establishment cleanliness, screaming children, inattentive service, food poisoning, corked wine, and the increase of credit card fraud. Regarding the last point, there seems to be an unspoken code among waitstaff in one particular U.S. city, where waiters often add an additional tip to the credit card charge slip after the patron has left. In an informal survey of ten residents in this city, 100 percent had this experience happen to them. Add-ons ranged

Courtesy of Tourism Vancouver

anywhere from a couple of dollars to more than USD 40 in one instance. Diners fought back by writing out the dollar value of the tip on the line on the charge slip instead of using numbers (e.g., "FIFTEEN" instead of "$15.00"). Why should diners have to fight? Simply put, they should not.

Destinations are starting to take quality of service in their hospitality industry very seriously. The Canadian province of British Columbia has set the world standard for customer service training with its SuperHost® workshops. Developed in 1985 to welcome the world for Expo '86 (held in Vancouver), the SuperHost® program is now a series of eight workshops designed for front-line staff and managers. Workshop contents can be customized and sessions are delivered by certified trainers in an interactive and informative learning environment. The original one-day program focuses on three key purposes: (1) Offering core skills for dealing effectively with people (like creating positive first impressions); (2) providing accurate information to our visitors and customers; and (3) understanding the importance of tourism in our local economy. This core program is also licensed in a number of destinations around the world, including Alaska (AlaskaHost); Australia (AussieHost); New Zealand (KiwiHost); England, Wales, Scotland and Northern Ireland (Welcome Host); Singapore (SuperHost® Singapore); Hong Kong (Hong Kong WonderHost); Thailand (SawasdeeHost); Philippines (Mabuhay Host) and Puerto Rico (Puerto Rico SuperHost®).

Holly Frederickson, Master Trainer for the SuperHost® program, says, "We want our graduates to leave our workshops equipped with knowledge and then apply that learning along with their existing experience. As ambassadors for their business and community, they create memorable experiences that influence whether or not someone will do repeat business or visit their area again. SuperHost® training is a critical component for the success of our industry." More information is available at http://www.tourismbc.com/superhost.

Great food can be served anywhere, but it is the interaction with the server that will make or break the experience. Regynald Washington, former Vice President and General Manager for Disney Regional Entertainment, summed it up most eloquently, "Good service can save a bad meal, but a great meal cannot save bad service."

Businesses must also make good on their claims. Consider a brewery that says it offers tours, even though the tour merely consists of a small group standing around looking at the beer fermenting vat. The group will not be satisfied. One group that I personally hosted in California was taken to a cheesemaker, only to discover the owner was late for the engagement. When he arrived, he was unkempt and clearly inexperienced with handling visitors. He thoroughly embarrassed himself, his businesses and his destination. Perhaps more than other tourists, Culinary Tourists must be satisfied with their experience. The reputation of the business and ultimately that of the destination is at stake.

SUCCESS

Destinations can become victims of their own success as they exceed their carrying capacity. Too much success leads to overgrowth and the debasement of a destination, all for the sake of making more money. California's Napa Valley is one such destination that has lost much of its allure and become a kind of theme park for wine tourism. Traffic jams on the country roads of Napa are now de rigueur. In fact, on any Saturday evening during the summer, it can take up to six hours to drive back to San Francisco from Napa (normally a 90-minute drive). Visitors spend most of that time sitting on the highway or waiting in the toll line to cross the Oakland Bridge. Do not expect any bargains at the Napa wineries either, where bottles regularly *start* at a shocking USD 75 (although cheaper bottles can occasionally be found). You will need more than just pocket change for the tastings in Napa as well, where

Outdoor reception at Henry Estate Winery in Oregon.

fees range on average from USD 2 to 15 *per taste (not per tasting)*. To be fair to the producers, sampling fees help reduce free-loading abuse and help defray product cost. The ultimate affront to the eager Napa tourist is the "Open by Appointment Only" signs that are proudly displayed on the gates of almost every other vineyard. This leaves significant promotional opportunity for lesser known, and perhaps more welcoming, destinations.

Many wineries do not agree that visitors should be charged tasting fees. Jim Trezise, Director of the New York Wine & Grape Foundation, shares that "wineries in New York State have total flexibility to determine whether to charge for samples at their tasting rooms, and the amount if they choose to do so. Most do not charge for a basic tasting, but an increasing number are offering visitors options involving different numbers and types of wine for which they charge fees. Others will charge for the tasting, but that amount is refunded with the purchase of wine, which is a reasonable way to ensure that the wine used for sampling is an investment with a return rather than just 'free booze.' Some charge for an 'Uncork New York' wine glass with their winery logo on the other side, which after the tasting the consumer takes home and which for the winery helps cover the cost of the samples. In short, wineries use different methods to balance the need to attract and please consumers without taking an unacceptable loss from wine samples. In New York, which has 219 wineries in five regions, the number of visitors increased by 54% in three years (2000–2003) to 4.14 million, and the per visitor spending increased 49% to USD 20.50, with wine accounting for 87% of total sales and gift items 13%. The wine industry is the fastest growing industry in New York's two largest economic sectors of agriculture and tourism, and has been the driving force in promoting agri-tourism and culinary tourism as well."

Success also means that some smaller businesses may become attractive takeover targets of larger businesses. For example, Vincor, Canada's largest wine producer and the fourth largest producer in North America, purchased popular Hogue Cellars in the U.S. state of Washington in August 2001. In August of 1999, Chalone Wine Group of Napa, California, USA, purchased the much smaller Staton Hills Winery in Wapato, Washington, USA. In May 2002, Gordon Brothers Cellars in Pasco, Washington, USA, was sold to the larger Freemark Abbey Winery, based in Napa Valley, California, USA. The fate of smaller winemakers seems to be falling more into the hands of the large corporations, with both positive and negative implications.

Culinary Tourism supports small, often family-run, businesses like restaurants and wineries. However, larger companies bring some benefits, the most noteworthy of which are investment capital, business experience, staff and media connections. Yet the goals of larger corporations generally go against those of smaller producers. Smaller producers tend to focus on their quality of life, which includes their families. They are artisans and are generally in the business because of a passion for what they do. Ultimately, the consolidation of smaller businesses to save money and production time bodes for loss of style and uniqueness, repression of creativity and loss of the personal touch that makes a culinary destination noteworthy and alluring in the first place. Smaller producers and destination management professionals should take note.

The degree to which large corporations influence (negatively or positively) winery management and wine style, restaurant management, and destination development, and whether that has any positive or negative impact on Culinary Tourism, is a topic worthy of further research.

GOVERNMENT REGULATIONS

Land use restrictions in many places restrain growth, such as in the states of Oregon, USA, and South Australia, Australia. Urban growth boundaries and land usage regulations can prevent or delay new construction or changes in land use. In some destinations, there is little or no room to grow. In others, strict building codes prevent building additions or modifications without considerable effort and cost. Small businesses rarely have the time, money or inclination to follow the ever-changing myriad government regulations. An environment of strict government regulations often favors larger businesses with more spending power. Destinations are urged to perform an impact assessment of the regulatory environment as part of their Culinary Tourism development strategy.

EDUCATION

There is an ongoing struggle over who will pay the bill to develop Culinary Tourism. In the United States, restaurants tend to see themselves in the food and beverage business and nothing more. Wineries and breweries see themselves as manufacturers. Shops see themselves as retailers. Businesses in more tourism-aware countries such as Australia, France and Italy tend to be much more aware of tourism's role in their business. More often than not, few businesses recognize their potential as part of the local tourism industry. "A significant number of winery owners/operators come from an agricultural and wine making background and have limited understanding of the dynamics of the tourism industry."[31] For example, "one-half of the members of the Napa Valley Vintners' Association appear not to recognize the importance of tourism."[32] This creates a problem when wineries or restaurants are approached to participate in a cooperative marketing program, for example. Even if there is no cost to participate, the food/beverage providers will likely dismiss the opportunity because they do not readily see how it fits in with their business. However, they may agree as long as the DMO pays for the promotions. There is a lot of work ahead to educate food and beverage producers and providers as to their role in tourism.

PUBLIC AWARENESS

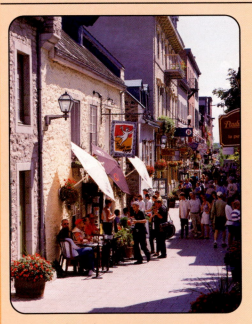

Local governments and the public both need to be educated about the importance of tourism, and especially Culinary Tourism, if the destination's goal is to succeed at attracting tourists. Residents and community leaders may physically see tourists on their streets, but how many of them appreciate that the lodging tax paid by tourists goes to fund schools and pave the roads? DMOs need a strategy for Culinary Tourism development that includes community outreach and awareness building. Perhaps most importantly, the general public needs to see an immediate, tangible economic impact of Culinary Tourism or support will likely wane.

Courtesy of Quebec City Tourism

[31]"Strategy for Wine and Culinary Tourism in Ontario: Background Report," Economic Planning Group of Canada, March 2001, p. 46.
[32]Ibid., p. 55.

What the Future Holds

As the Culinary Tourism niche matures, and as more professionals begin to understand its role within their local tourism industry, we will likely see more food and wine tour routes; more food-oriented travel guidebooks; more focus on travel in food magazines; and more itineraries that celebrate food/drink as an integral part of the travel experience. Already, Zagat's, a popular restaurant rating guide in the US, has organized its listings by city. There may be an opportunity for publishers such as Zagat's to weave general editorial commentary about destinations into their ratings, which can help to shape popular opinion and influence travel decisions.

Within individual businesses, look for refinements in style and service upgrades. Establishments that suddenly find themselves in a Culinary Tourism region will likely upgrade their facilities and some may have to train their staffs in order to meet the service and experience expectations of Culinary Tourists.

As Culinary Tourism grows, business owners and destination marketers will notice more opportunity for partnerships. The matrix in Figure 3 (page 48) gives an idea of the types of Culinary Tourism partnerships that are likely to be successful.

Some wineries and breweries have already demonstrated an appreciation for Culinary Tourism. DMOs have just begun to discover the importance of Culinary Tourism. DMOs and businesses with a viable product offering would be well served to beat emerging competition and begin to research the viability of integrating a Culinary Tourism strategy into their strategic planning.

Merchandising opportunities hold additional future potential. A case study can be found in Oregon, USA, where Your Northwest and Made in Oregon operate several retail stores. Made in Oregon proudly claims "All products made, caught or grown in Oregon." Both stores sell locally made and grown products that include regional wines, beers, berry preserves/jam, hazelnut products, and even coffee.[33] A Made in Oregon store at the Portland International Airport gives visitors one last chance to stock up on any Oregon wines before their flight.

---

[33]For more information, visit http://www.yournw.com and http://www.madeinoregon.com

	Restaurant	Winery	Café	Bar	Farm	Market	Event	Tour route	Lodging	Retail
Restaurant		•		•	•		•	•	•	•
Winery	•			•			•	•	•	•
Café				•		•	•			•
Bar	•	•	•				•			
Farm	•					•	•	•	•	•
Market			•		•		•			•
Event	•	•	•	•	•	•	•		•	
Tour route	•	•			•				•	
Lodging	•	•			•		•	•		
Retail	•	•	•		•	•				

The chart shows various culinary tourism components. The dots show the intersections of the business partnerships with the highest chance of success.

Figure 3   Culinary Tourism partnership matrix.

Smaller, less commercial venues such as farms and orchards have the opportunity to capitalize on a similar merchandising opportunity. Such retail operations should take a hint from the National Wine Centre of Australia and offer to ship as much as possible (or as is legal) for visitors. Who wants to carry around a half-dozen heavy wine bottles, or a case of strawberry preserve jars, or bags of chocolate-covered hazelnuts that will melt? Visitors who can ship products home at a fair price are also likely to spend more per purchase than if they had to carry the items home with them.

Culinary Tourists, who are arguably more affluent than many other kinds of tourists, expect to be able to pay by credit card. Customers also tend to spend more per purchase when they can charge the purchase on their credit card. Smaller producers and smaller destinations should take note.

Culinary Tourism is a new niche that holds great potential for community economic development and improvement of quality of life. When tourists fill otherwise empty restaurant tables, more sales are made and more waitstaff are required. More sales means more profit and more capital to spend and reinvest in the community. Tourists stay longer and spend more nights in hotel rooms, which earns local gov-

Oregon lies just above California, on the West coast of the United States, and is located on the same temperate 45th latitude as Burgundy, France. Its climate is blessed with a long growing season, fertile soil and abundant rain. Strict land use regulations protect smaller farm producers. Oregon is also the third largest wine-producing state in the United States.

ernments more room tax than they normally would receive. This spending helps support community services such as road repair, sewage and garbage collection. These services benefit the residents much more than visitors.

Culinary Tourism holds potential for both urban and rural destinations. Before Culinary Tourism will take hold, however, the destination or business must have a unique product or service that will attract the Culinary Tourist explorers.

On a final note, owners of cafés, delis or otherwise mundane establishments should not feel that their place of business would not be of interest to Culinary Tourists. The previous example of Culinary Tourists enjoying the quintessential British pub or watching the French cheesemaker still stands. Culinary Tourists are interested in unique, memorable experiences, not just experiences of a four-star nature. Chains and quick service establishments can also benefit from a greater number of culinary tourists.

This book has uncovered a number of opportunities for future research:

- How to best educate food and beverage professionals as to their impact on, and role within, the tourism industry
- The degree to which Culinary Tourists from various countries share similar demographic and psychographic traits
- Motivations of diners and Culinary Tourists
- The degree to which product sampling affects tourists' knowledge, and recollection, of local food and drink
- The economic impact of Culinary Tourism on foreign trade balance
- The degree to which cuisine promotes cross-cultural awareness and understanding
- The role of food and drink in international and cross-cultural communication
- The economic impact of food/beverage event visitors on local communities
- The degree to which large corporations influence (negatively or positively) winery management and wine style, restaurant management, and destination development, and whether their influence has any positive or negative impact on Culinary Tourism
- The environmental impact of Culinary Tourists on small towns vs. large cities

The goal of this book is to prove to food, beverage and travel professionals throughout the world that Culinary Tourism is an important new niche and worthy of attention. Hopefully this book has provoked thought, incited discussion, increased industry knowledge and moved professionals to find ways to include Culinary Tourism in future product development and marketing strategies.

This book is a starting point on which to build. Future books will discuss how to design a Culinary Tourism strategy and how to design and implement a Culinary Tourism marketing plan.

NEXT STEPS

Food is the last component of the visitor experience that still holds potential for further development. Perhaps because we eat so often, we have overlooked the importance of food to the visitor. Recognizing the importance of food to a positive visitor experience is the first step a destination or business must take before it develops a Culinary Tourism strategy. Once that is acknowledged, senior management must buy into the concept before any development begins, as is the case with most product development. Culinary Tourism is a new industry and an unchartered course. There is no need to venture down the Culinary Tourism development road alone. Please consult the inside back cover for ways how the International Culinary Tourism Association can help promote economic and community development in your area.

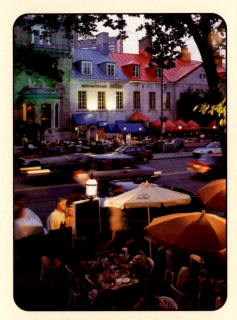

Courtesy of Quebec City Tourism

BIBLIOGRAPHY

The International Culinary Tourism Association offers an exclusive members-only online resource portal where members can view and download Culinary Tourism research, best practices studies, sample marketing plans, promotional collateral and general articles. To join the Association visit http://www.culinarytourism.org.

Additional noteworthy reading includes:

"Acquiring a Taste for Cuisine Tourism: A Product Development Strategy," Canadian Tourism Commission, Ottawa, Ontario, Canada, June 2002.

Clarke, Heather L. "Wine and Culinary Tourism in Australia," Prepared for the Ontario Ministry of Tourism, Culture and Recreation, March 2001.

Getz, Donald. "Explore Wine Tourism: Management, Development and Destinations," *Cognizant Communications,* 2000.

Hall, C. Michael, ed. *Food Tourism Around The World : Development, Management and Markets,* Butterworth-Heinemann, September 30, 2003.

"The Marketing Decade: Setting the Australian Wine Marketing Agenda 2000 >> 2010," Winemakers' Federation of Australia and Australian Wine and Brandy Corporation.

Moore, Margaret. "Restaurants that Represent the Essence of Charleston and the South Carolina Low Country," excerpt from *Complete Charleston—A Guide to the Architecture, History & Gardens of Charleston and the Low Country,* date unavailable.

Poised for Greatness, A Strategic Framework for the Ontario Wine Industry, including Appendices.

"Profile of Sonoma County Visitors," Menlo Consulting Group, Santa Rosa, California, July 12, 1999.

Sonnenfeld, Albert, ed. "Food: A Culinary History from Antiquity to the Present," English edition, Columbia University Press, 1999.

"Sonoma County Tourism Program, Strategic Marketing Plan, July 1, 2001—June 30, 2002," Sonoma County Chamber of Commerce.

"Sonoma County Travel Impacts," Data Sheet, Sonoma County Chamber of Commerce, March 28, 2002.

"A Strategy for Wine and Culinary Tourism in Ontario, Background Report," Economic Planning Group of Canada, March 2001.

"Tourism Tasmania Wine Survey 2000," www.tourism.tas.gov.au

"Travel Activities & Motivation Survey (TAMS), Wine & Cuisine Report," Lang Research, March 2001.

ABBREVIATIONS

ATC   Australian Tourist Commission

AUD   Australian Dollar

B&B   Bed & Breakfast, (type of accommodation)

CTC   Canadian Tourism Commission

CVB   Convention & Visitors Bureau

DMO   Destination Marketing Organization

F&B   Food & Beverage

FIT   Foreign Independent Traveler and/or Frequent Individual Tourist. Various permutations of this term are used to differentiate an individual traveler from a group traveler.

ROE   Rate of exchange (for foreign exchange rates)

USD   U.S. Dollar

ABOUT THE AUTHOR

Erik Wolf hails from humble roots in America's heartland, the Midwest state of Nebraska. Erik studied languages at the University of Virginia and Travel Marketing and International Communication at the American University in Washington, D.C. While spending four years in D.C., Erik worked at Meridian International Center as a meeting planner, arranging programs for visiting international business and government leaders. After an internship at the former U.S. Travel and Tourism Administration in Sydney, Australia, Erik moved to New York City, where he served as Director of Sales and Marketing for Domenico Tours, then the third largest tour operator in the United States.

When Domenico closed its doors, Erik launched Big Blue Marble, his own marketing communications firm in New York. He serviced several top-tier clients, including two divisions of American Express, where he helped to launch an electronic ticketing technology system. He also helped to overhaul the company's consumer marketing process. While based in New York, Erik found time to orchestrate international charity events in New York, Greece and Australia. He also taught travel marketing to undergraduate students at New York University. After six years in New York, Erik left to join the San Francisco office of Ion Global, a Hong Kong-based information technology consulting firm. There he led technology integration and marketing projects for MCI WorldCom, Walt Disney and other travel and food industry clients. Finally, in 2001, Erik left San Francisco to settle down in beautiful Portland, Oregon.

Erik has been a Culinary Tourist his entire life. In the course of his travels to 45 countries on 5 continents, in addition to the occasional restaurant, he has eaten at roadside vendors, delis, bakeries and in people's homes. For Erik, food is a way to communicate and connect intimately with local people. Many destinations offer travelers compelling value propositions in the form of truly unique food and beverage experiences, which led to Erik's passion for Culinary Tourism.

Today Erik enjoys recommending obscure but affordable wines from far-off lands to his friends. A word of warning: Don't ever let him loose in a grocery store in another country—you won't see him for hours.

How Culinary Tourism Benefits You

Food and beverage are an equally—if not more—powerful tourism allure than attractions like culture, sports and shopping. If you doubt it, just look at your own behavior when you travel. You can eat and drink anywhere, anytime, no matter the weather or season. To dine is to enjoy the only art form involving all five human senses, enhancing the chance a visitor will remember a meal more than a museum visit. The potential of food and drink to generate far-reaching word-of-mouth promotion is greater than that of any other visitor attraction.

The Association's Mission

The mission of the International Culinary Tourism Association is to help food and beverage manufacturers and providers, as well as travel industry professionals, to package and promote their culinary treasures as marketable and sellable attractions.

How the International Culinary Tourism Association (ICTA) Helps You

The ICTA accomplishes its goals through education and networking activities such as Culinary Tourism summits, symposia and consulting work; providing extensive resources in our members-only online Culinary Tourism knowledge portal; and pioneering cooperative marketing activities such as Culinary Tourism guidebooks, websites and newsletters targeting both the trade and consumers.

Newsletter

Sign up for our free CuisineScene[SM] newsletter—get monthly updates about what's hot and fresh in the Culinary Tourism industry. More details at **www.culinarytourism.org/newsletter.**

Memberships

Join today to take advantage of the Association's unique education and networking resources for you and your business. Specifics at **www.culinarytourism.org/membership.**

Education

The Association realizes its goals largely through its education and networking. Some details below, with more information online at **www.culinarytourism.org/education.**

- **Regional Symposia**—One day mini-conference with five intense general sessions covering specific topics of direct relevance to regional businesses. Explore upcoming symposia regions, dates and programs in the Education section of our website.

- **BrainFood[SM]**—All members receive free access to the world's largest online library of culinary tourism resources and industry research, including marketing plans, marketing collateral, industry best practices, marketing campaigns, product development examples, media coverage, audio interviews and much, much more.

- **Seminars**—

  ❶ **Culinary Tourism: The Hidden Harvest**—*(see and hear the book come alive in this introductory session), either as a keynote or individual session. Why not treat each attendee to a copy of this book as a valuable reference guide.*

  ❷ **Baking the Cake: A Recipe for Culinary Tourism Product Development**

  ❸ **Feast or Famine: Best Practices in Culinary Tourism Marketing**

- **Summits**—Full day interactive workshops for your organization, constituents, members, or leadership. The day ends with a recipe, or roadmap, for Culinary Tourism development in your community.

- **Speakers Bureau**—Are you looking for a specific knowledge matter expert on food, beverage, hospitality or tourism? More than likely we have the person you seek among our vast list of industry contacts.

- **Culinary Tourism: The Hidden Harvest.** Order more copies of this book for your members, leadership or conference delegates. Log on to www.culinarytourism.org/book for volume discounts and ordering information.